IRISH BLOOD, ENGLISH HEART

Darren Murphy

IRISH BLOOD, ENGLISH HEART

OBERON BOOKS
LONDON

WWW.OBERONBOOKS.COM

First published in 2011 by Oberon Books Ltd
521 Caledonian Road, London N7 9RH

A catalogue record for this book is available from the British Library.

ISBN: 978-1-84943-094-4

Cover image by Alex Sargent

Ancient Lights, a new collective of London writers, actors, directors and designers, was established in 2010, to unearth the dominion of stories that lie buried within the stones, strata, and surfaces of London streets. The capital is both a city of mongrel influences and an international cultural hub, peopled by disparate citizens and cultures; unique, indomitable and fierce. *Ancient Lights* is a restless camera that illuminates these forgotten, unlit corners of an ageless, pulsating, raging city. We tell London stories.

For Mum and Dad.

And for Ian, Howard, Carolyn, and Caitriona,
for that conversation we had last summer over a pint in The Ring.

Irish Blood, English Heart was first produced at the Union Theatre, Southwark on 15th February 2011, by the Ancient Lights Theatre Co.

CON SWEENEY, Ian Groombridge
PEGGY SWEENEY, Carolyn Tomkinson
RAY SUEDE, Howard Teale
ANTHONY KANE, Oliver Gilbert

Directed by Caitriona McLaughlin
Assistant director Daniel Hughes
Designed by Francesca Rodrigues
Movement direction by Clare McKenna
Artwork & publicity design by Spiff
Stage management Elizabeth Mansfield
Lighting by Steve Miller

This production subsequently transferred to the Trafalgar Studios on 2nd May 2011, with the same cast, and with the following changes:

Lighting design by Phil Spenser Hunter
Sound design by Bertram Knappitsch
Assistant director Kanika Clayton
Stage management Cosmo Cooper
Press Officer Cliona Roberts
Produced by Jo Hole

Characters

CON SWEENEY

PEGGY SWEENEY

RAY SUEDE

ANTHONY KANE

A late afternoon in spring.

A lock-up garage-come-makeshift-storage room in Southwark, south London. It is large, spacious, dusty. The space doesn't seem to have a specific function and could be a warehouse or a readymade gym or a small improvised theatre. At the moment it is none of these things, it is merely a large, empty space. Dusty boxes and crates containing various items of undisclosed purpose occupy the back wall, which is dominated by a large map of London. A smaller, arcane map of Ireland is alongside it. A cheap CD player sits on a cheap coffee table, a stack of CDs in a cardboard box alongside it.

Centre stage is the wreck of an old, decrepit, and disused black London cab. It is lopsided as the two tyres on the left hand side are punctured. The paintwork is flayed and peeling, and there are obvious signs of rust and neglect. A teddy bear mascot has been roughly attached by string to the front of the bonnet, weatherbeaten and shorn of fur.

A single plastic chair in front of it. A shillelagh hangs on a hook by the door. A plaid jacket hangs on a wire coat hanger on a nail driven into a bit of timber.

ACT ONE

CON SWEENEY, a 38-year-old, Walworth born, ex-London cabbie in smart casuals, is alone. He is in the process of packing. He holds a small palm-sized video camera, which he slowly pans around the room, coming to rest on the cab. He puts the camera down on the table.

He crouches on his haunches, rifling through the stack of CDs on the floor. He selects one at random, inserts it into the CD player and plays it. It plays The Streets' Sharp Darts. *He looks confused. He ejects it and chucks it onto the pile of rejected CDs on the floor, continues rifling through the pile. Two items in the shoebox catch his attention: a small trophy, and a faded mass card. He takes them out and sets them to one side. He selects another CD. This time it's an old scratchy recording of the prologue from* Henry V, *spoken by* Emrys James. *It startles him momentarily, then a small smile of recognition. As it progresses he mouths some of the words to himself, though remembering few:*

CHORUS
  O for a muse of fire, that would ascend
  The brightest heaven of invention;
  A kingdom for a stage, princes to act
  And monarchs to behold the swelling scene!
  Then should the warlike Harry, like himself
  Assume the port of Mars; and at his heels,
  Leash'd in like hounds, should famine, sword and fire
  Crouch for employment. But pardon, gentles all,
  The flat unraised spirits that have dared
  On this unworthy scaffold to bring forth
  So great an object: can this cockpit hold
  The vasty fields of France? Or may we cram
  Within this wooden O the very casques
  That did afright the air at Agincourt?
  O, pardon –

He switches it off, ejects it, and carefully replaces it to one side in the 'good' pile. He selects another: My Lagan Love, *sung by Margaret Barry. He lets this play, picking up the trophy and mass card and standing.*

He peers at the inscription on the trophy, then at the mass card, which he turns over to read. He slowly scans the room, and places the mass card on the coffee table.

PEGGY SWEENEY, his wife, enters, agitated. She is 40. She carries a handbag, which she places on the table.

PEGGY: Had to go up to…what's it called? Towards the Borough. The car park off America street. *(She picks up the mass card.)*

CON: Hawkins said he'd be in here for hours sometimes, on his jack, listening to this stuff. Dad used to say you could tell who all the plastic paddies were in the Irish pubs, they were the ones who knew all of the words to *The Fields of Athenry* and sang the rebel songs louder than anyone else.

PEGGY: *(Noticing camera on table.)* Didn't know you brought the camera.

CON: Thought the girls might be interested. Later on.

PEGGY: You reckon?

CON: Look at this place. It's like Aladdin's cave. He shrank London down to the size of a lock up in Southwark. That's worth recording, ennit? Before Hawkins tears it down.

PEGGY: Well, I got Gemma's birthday on that, so don't go over it. *(Reading the mass card.)* September 3rd, 1953. Philomena Corcoran. Who's Philomena Corcoran?

CON: Name rings a bell but I couldn't quite place her.

PEGGY: Your mum said he was a bit of a ladies man. *(She hands it back.)* Before her, I mean. *(He puts it back in the shoebox. She turns the CD down.)* Ray's definitely coming?

CON: He just texted, he's on his way. Know what the old man told me once? Said he was a Londoner before he was anything else. He was a Mullingar thoroughbred, but he had to *earn* the right to be called a proper Londoner, way he saw it. Had to work at it. Out every evening on his bike, after grafting all day on the hod, learning his routes.

Imagine learning that blue book inside out, and holding down a job like that, *and* starting a family. 320 routes, 25000 streets. On his bike, hail or shine, after work, for four years. When he got his Green Badge he said: Now I'm a Londoner.

PEGGY: You did it too, Con.

CON: Not like him.

PEGGY: But you did it. Got your badge.

CON: It's like he got off that boat train at Euston and thought: I'm gonna have this. Like he looked at the tube map and just swallowed it whole. Just cos he decided he could. Sheer, blind, driving will. He had that… that steel, y'know? That generation weren't born, they were constructed from leftover bits of RSJs. Now, you tell me how a man like that…

He is staring at the cab. A silence.

PEGGY: Ray *owes* us. Look, I spoke to the woman today about the studio space. If Ray gives us a cheque today she said we can get the application in tonight and pay it in first thing in the morning. It'll secure the space until it clears.

CON: I told you, I can't decide for him.

PEGGY: *(Turning CD off.)* Then decide for us. Decide for the girls.

CON: Bit below the belt, isn't it, Peg?

PEGGY: But then why ask him here?

CON: I told you. To show him this place. Before Hawkins rents it out again.

PEGGY: This place?

CON: The man was still our father. He came to this country with nothing.

PEGGY: So? They all did then.

CON: It counts for something. So what then, another handout from Ray? Is that how we're living now? On blood money?

PEGGY: We wouldn't have to ask him for handouts if he paid us what he owes. The property officer at Iliffe yard said those studio spaces are really adaptable and –

CON: I told you, Peg –

PEGGY: She said we could split the space, and put up a partition wall. We could start small. It's not quite the restaurant we'd talked about, but there's loads of businesses round there, you could have a take away menu to begin with, and I could use part of the space for –

CON: I don't wanna talk about it.

PEGGY: We *haven't* talked about it. We've talked about how we're *not* gonna talk about it.

CON: Then I don't wanna talk about not talking about it. He's my brother.

PEGGY: And I'm your wife. If it's not in by seven we lose it.

CON looks at her a moment, then looks away. He looks at the trophy he is still holding and peers at the inscription.

CON: Cross country, Mullingar, under-12s. 1949. First place. Funny, I can't see him running, can you? That swagger he had.

PEGGY is staring at him. He catches her and crosses to the other side of the room. He places the trophy carefully back in the shoebox with the CDs. He looks up. She is still staring at him.

PEGGY: He owes us, Con. Everything he said in the book, everything he wrote about you…

CON: Like he told us: it wasn't about –

PEGGY: He made you sound like an idiot!

CON: He explained all that. It's just a character Ray plays onstage…

PEGGY: That just happens to sound exactly like you.

CON: The character in the book was just an *amalgam* of different people he remembers when he was –

PEGGY: O, for Christ's sake grow up, Con. You actually believe that? That its a mash up of people he met on the circuit when he was doing stand up? You can be so *naive.*

CON: It's simply a way for him to… process everything that happened to him, through this character who –

PEGGY: Just so happens to be a second generation Irish London cabbie the same age as you, who just so happens to live in Lewisham, and just so happens to be married to a thundering bitch…

CON: That's not supposed to be you…

PEGGY: She's got red hair! Stop being so fucking *reasonable.* The moronic, neurotic, psychotic couple, it's us. Everybody we know knows that. *(Beat.)* This is our chance, Con. Everything we talked about. The restaurant. Something to leave the girls. Something for us. Con?

CON: I know. And it's a nice thought.

PEGGY: We could do it with twenty thousand and –

CON: Twenty?

PEGGY: If we borrowed against the mortgage, got a start up loan. I've looked into it, I got some brochures from the start up initiative, the bloke from Lewisham council said –

CON: You want to ask Ray for twenty thousand?

PEGGY: It's nothing.

CON: It's not nothing, Peg.

PEGGY: He pays twice that in taxes.

CON: Twenty thousand pounds is not nothing. He wrote a book, Peg.

PEGGY: He mocked us. He belittled our lives, Con, he belittled you. He's laughing at you, and he's not even doing it behind your back. He's doing a tour!

CON: And he should pay for that?

PEGGY: Yes! He's got that deal with the TV networks in the States, they're turning the book into a series. Believe me, he won't even miss it.

CON: I can't.

PEGGY: You mean you won't.

CON: I'll find something. I'm doing my best, alright?

PEGGY: Your best doesn't even come close. Your best doesn't even cover new school uniforms for the girls. Your best is only trying to repair the damage you wreaked on our family, Con. We'll be lucky if we hold onto the house at this rate. Think about that next time you…

CON: Next time I what?

PEGGY: *(Turns away.)* I'm gonna finish up out the –

CON: Next time I what, Peggy?

She goes out the back door towards the kitchen and bathroom. CON goes over to the black cab. He lightly runs a finger along the rust on the front wheel arch. PEGGY can be heard aggressively cleaning up out back.

With a slight sense of trespassing, he climbs into the front seat behind the steering wheel. He surveys the room before gently resting his forehead lightly on the wheel. PEGGY re-enters carrying a half empty litre bottle of whiskey and a bin bag.

PEGGY: That's the last of the – *(She spots him, and is rooted to the spot.)* Jesus Christ, Con…

CON: What?

PEGGY: Don't sit like that. With your head…y'know?

CON: Oh. Yeah. Sorry. *(He climbs out.)* Hawkins told me when I picked up the keys that they'd be here six hours a day, five days a week. Mainly afternoons, evenings.

PEGGY: Him and the kid?

CON: Anthony. Hawkins came in one time, he said, and the kid was behind the wheel, calling out the names of the streets and places of interest. Dad was just stood there, eyes closed, mouthing them. Like a prayer. Never even heard him come in.

PEGGY: *(Walking over to the cab.)* Must've been a shock. When Hawkins found him.

She spots something on the floor of the cab. She leans in to retrieve it: an old paperback. She flicks through it, and a small faded newspaper clipping falls out.

CON: Like he was playing a game, he said. Like he was holding his breath.

She picks up the clipping, reads it.

CON: We've got til six, he said. We can leave the keys in the box downstairs.

PEGGY: *(Reading.)* 'The inquest was held today into the death of Philomena Corcoran, an 18-year-old woman of Mullingar, Westmeath, who was found drowned in the Royal canal. She was discovered by James McKilvanney, who was out walking his dog early on the morning of 1st September.'

CON: Show.

She hands it to him. He reads it.

PEGGY: Ray's tour schedule sounded pretty hectic. I think he'd be here by now, if he was coming. Maybe we should just finish up and –

CON: *(Reading.)* 'It appeared that Ms. Corcoran had caught her foot in some wire that had worked itself loose from the fence that cordoned off the canal, and had slipped down the bank into the water. She had knocked herself out on the metal filter that was set into the bank and had failed to regain consciousness. A verdict of accidental death was returned.'

PEGGY: Why did he keep that?

CON: *(Placing the clipping in the paperback and placing it in the shoebox.)* I think they were friends, the three of them. Mum said... oh, I forget now...

PEGGY: You know Ray's flight's at nine, Con? He has to allow himself two hours for –

CON: He was still his father. He'll see it different when he comes. If – when – the kid tells him.

PEGGY: You can't reconstruct him from fragments, Con, from old mass cards and clippings and trophies. You can't make Ray remember it different to how he remembers it. Ray's not you.

CON: He proved it. In here he proved it.

PEGGY: Ray might not see it that way.

CON: He will. When I show him. When the kid...

PEGGY: Okay, Con. Okay. Let's just try and be out by half past. *(Beat.)* Why does he still call himself that anyway? It's not just a stage name is it? 'Ray Suede'. Sounds like a lounge lizard. Or a Seventies porn star.

CON: Don't you remember? That night in *The Crown*. At the birth of Ray Suede. In Willesden. We're sitting there, belting down pints of Fosters when suddenly Ray, yeah, Ray just grabs my packet of B&H and sets it down next to the box of matches. Then he moves around the ashtray and the beermat, and out of nothing he's conjuring this mad little scene in front of us. He starts performing this little, I dunno, voodoo *ritual.* And suddenly he's this MC, and he's introducing all of the turns. So, each item on the table represents a different act. The B&H pack is a

Venezuelan snake charmer with different coloured glass eyes…

ANTHONY, 21, a man from the local area, comes in, hovering uncertainly by the entrance to the room.

And the box of Bryant & May matches is a ventriloquist from Merton. Ray went into a trance. You were killing yourself. He was at it for two hours. I think you wet yourself a little.

PEGGY: What?

CON: Just a bit.

PEGGY: Piss off.

CON: Not much. You just did a little pee.

PEGGY: What was I, five? I never wet myself. What the hell are you talking about?

CON spots ANTHONY.

CON: Yes, mate? Can I…?

ANTHONY: It's alright, I'll come back.

He goes, hurriedly. The street door slams. After a beat CON remembers.

CON: Shit. That's him. Should I…?

He is torn between staying and going. PEGGY moves towards the door.

PEGGY: I'll go. Wait here in case Ray comes.

She goes. The street door slams. CON is staring at the door.

He goes to the map of Ireland and looks at it. Then he goes to the pile of CDs and begins rifling through them. He selects one, inserts it, and plays: Hank Williams' Ramblin' Man.

He glances at his watch and goes off left, towards the toilet. The stage is empty for a moment, reverberating to Hank Williams' keening lament. The street door opens, off.

RAY SUEDE enters. He is wheeling a small Samsonite suitcase and is very smartly attired in a chic, expensive, beautifully cut, but understated suit. He is 42, and has an unmistakable, but not showy, aura of success about him. He stops at the threshold of the room, staring at the cab.

The toilet flushes, off. RAY looks towards the door that leads to the bathroom, unconsciously straightening and preparing himself. CON enters, reading a paper. He glances up and stops on sight of RAY. They look at each other a long time without speaking.

RAY: I'm Sparticus.

Beat.

CON: No, I'm Sparticus.

RAY: No, I am.

CON: No, I am.

RAY: No, but I am.

Beat.

CON: No, really, I am.

RAY: No, you're *Spasticus.*

CON: Oh yeah, I forgot.

RAY: King Of The Stupids.

CON: Hail.

RAY: All hail.

CON: Whither thou, friend?

RAY: Up hill and down dale, hither and *yon.*

CON: Prithee, take thy rest, Easy Rider. Why so, suited and booted?

RAY: Well I –

CON: And come dressed in habiliments of *war*?

RAY: Like a two bob cunt, you mean?

CON: Your words, not mine.

RAY: I come to pay tribute.

CON: Thanks and praise. Speak thy brains, sir. 'Tis received kindly.

RAY: By another two bob cunt with a Mr. Topper haircut. *(Indicating CON's hair.)* 'Tis not so much should I part my hair to the side or in the middle, as to where should I stop with the flannel?

CON starts laughing, breaking the game.

CON: Nice whistle, bro. Seriously.

RAY: Came straight from a book signing. There was a Q & A afterwards and some press junket they'd set up at the Dorchester. It's my uniform.

CON: Never explain, never apologise.

RAY: That's right, mate. That's right. *(Going to him, embracing him. He stands back and looks at CON.)* You're looking fit, mate. Seriously fit.

CON: I started running.

RAY: You always hated running.

CON: I know.

RAY: You'd feign illness to get out of cross country.

CON: I'm doing the marathon next year, touch wood.

RAY: Good for you, mate. Good for you. How's Peggy?

CON: Good. She's just… she'll be here in a bit.

RAY: Lovely. Lovely. And the girls?

CON: Good. They're very good.

RAY: What're they now, Jenny must be –

CON: Gemma.

RAY: Gemma… she's… I get them the wrong way round, she's the… youngest?

CON: That's right.

RAY: And she's, what, four now?

CON: Six.

RAY: She's... is she really? When did that happen?

CON: It just... happened.

RAY: You didn't just replace the four year old with a six year old? Which makes... Hannah...

CON: Heather.

RAY: Heather, of course... what, ten?

CON: Eight.

RAY: Eight, right. Yes. *(RAY unzips the suitcase and takes out two giftwrapped parcels for the girls.)* Gemma; Saturday 4th, 2004, 3 a.m., difficult labour, 5 lbs. 3 oz, Heather; October 14th, 2002, surprisingly easy labour for a first, a very wet Wednesday, and a very healthy 9 lbs. Mate, I'm not gonna forget how old my favourite God daughters are, am I? *(Beat. They stare at each other.)* So.

CON: Here we are.

RAY: Yeah. Here we are.

CON, sorting through a box, pulls out a dusty VHS copy of The Quiet Man. *Grins. RAY indulges him with a smile. CON puts it in the 'to keep' box.*

CON: Oh, I saw the interview. This morning. Thought you came over very well.

RAY: Keep it light and fluffy my agent says. Daytime TV. It's Day-Glo. No subtle shading, no grey areas. Everyone runs around like they're on helium. *(Beat.)* It's not you, y'know? The character. I know the voice has a similar –

CON: You don't have to explain.

RAY: I'm not. It's just an amalgam of –

CON: Peggy thinks it is.

RAY: Does she?

CON: She thinks it's based on us.

RAY: It's not.

CON: I know.

RAY: If I thought, for a second that you believed that…

CON: I don't think it is. I've told her. She'll… she'll come round.

RAY: You think I would do that?

CON: What did I just say?

RAY: It's a… it's a comic fantasia, it's so obviously not a –

CON: Are you listening to me?

RAY: They keep saying this, I keep getting asked this in interviews, is it autobio –

CON: *Ray…*

RAY: The same stupid question, they don't even rephrase it…

CON: Ray! What did I just say? I just said I didn't think it was based on us. I just said that. Peggy's just… you didn't have to give the wife red hair.

RAY: Yeah, that… *that* I regret. It's coincidental, by the way. And I'm gonna insist they change it for the TV series. Y'know, they never credit you with having any imagination, the Yanks, for the sheer inventiveness of storytelling. They think that if you come from London and your brother's a cabbie and you write a story about a London cabbie then ergo they must be one and the same person. Where'd you get your ideas from, they go. Well, I just sit and think them up, I say. Whilst having a shit.

CON: The muse comes upon you.

RAY: It does, mate, it does. They think I'm taking the piss. They think it all has to come from some deep well of your anguished interior life. Nice jacket, by the way. Very old school.

CON: Thanks. Are you still in the same place?

RAY: No. I moved. East 60th, between 2nd and 3rd. Midtown. About six blocks from Central Park.

CON: Is it "awesome"?

RAY: There's this… kinetic energy on the streets there that's just relentless… it's built into the sidewalks, it's in the architecture, it's in the way they serve the food. And if you're on top of it, if you're riding this wave of energy it's… The first tour, the readings, the launch, the chat shows… it just went ballistic. I blinked and three months had gone by. It's fun, for a bit. And the groupies! The creative writing students! But you can't do it for too long, it'll eat you alive. It'll start up again when they broadcast the series in the Fall.

CON: In the what?

RAY: Autumn, sorry. The absolutely latest I can be out of here is quarter to six. *(RAY carefully scans the room, as if itemising every object within it. CON is staring at him.)* You know, I nearly walked straight past this place. Smells like a church. What is that, candles?

CON: Found some in a box over there. Musta pinched 'em from St. Joseph's.

RAY: *(Notices CON looking at him.)* What?

CON: There is a certain… aura it gives off, isn't there? Success. A certain ease.

RAY: It's an illusion, mate. *(Beat. RAY holds his gaze a moment. He turns to the cab, regards it at length.)* Who found him?

CON: Mr. Hawkins. The landlord of the lock up. No ID, no wallet, nothing. Just this. *(He takes a faded polaroid from his jacket and hands it to RAY.)* That's all the police had to go on. The last place he lived in, the bedsit down the Elephant, they asked around but no one knew him. Kept himself to himself. No visitors.

RAY: That sounds like him alright.

CON: He'd been there just over two years. I'd never been. I used to see him at the old place, time to time.

RAY: What happened?

CON: We, well, we sorta fell out.

RAY: And you didn't know where he was?

CON: I... well, I...

RAY: Believe me, I know how cranky he could be, you don't have to explain.

CON: I was... it was stupid, I kept meaning to go round.

RAY: He woulda known that.

CON: So, all they had was this old photo. *(RAY looks at the photo.)* Your first holy communion. It's outside St. Joseph's. You remember it?

RAY: Not really. This was all he had on him? *(He crumples it, drops it to the floor.)*

CON: I left messages for you. E-mails...

RAY: I was on tour.

CON: You coulda phoned.

RAY: I didn't get them til I got back. Fifteen hundred unread e-mails to wade through. Not all you, obviously.

CON: I left a message with that... with the girl, your assis –

RAY: What did I just say, Con? My laptop was being serviced, we were on the road, we were touring.

CON: You couldn't have borrowed one?

RAY: There was no downtime, Con, it was a murderous schedule, you shoulda seen the itinerary I –

CON: You couldn't pick up a phone?

RAY: I was busy.

CON: That's nice.

RAY: You know what I mean. I was about to call you when you called me actually.

CON: Why didn't you call me at the time? I musta left fifty messages.

RAY: I was gonna call, I swear, I just... I had to get my head round it first.

CON: Six weeks.

RAY: I know.

CON: The funeral was six weeks ago.

RAY: What did you want me to do, drop everything?

CON: *(Exploding.)* He was your father.

RAY: I'm not a hypocrite, Con.

CON: You should've paid your respects.

RAY: Oh, and now I should genuflect and cross myself. Mea fucken Culpa.

CON: You're wrong about him, Ray.

RAY: I knew this was a mistake.

CON: So it was me and Peg at Nunhead cemetery, and the priest. On a day the colour of dishrags.

RAY: There was no one else at all?

CON: Not since Mum passed, no.

RAY: No one came from home?

CON: Home?

RAY: Y'know, Ireland.

CON: Why'd you call it that? He took us over for summer holidays when we were kids, but he hadn't been back in thirty years. He's been here over forty. How was it 'home'?

RAY: I don't think he saw it like that.

CON: How would you know?

RAY: They're his family.

CON: We're his family.

RAY: It weren't exactly the Waltons was it?

CON: They hadn't seen him in thirty years. I wasn't going to let them take over and have him laid out for three days in our living room whilst they turned his funeral into a festival of Kimberly biscuits, whiskey, and grief porn. *(Beat.)* Sorry. It's just been a a lot to take in. All this.

RAY: A secret den, eh?

CON: Yeah. How about that? Reason I... I had this idea we could... Bet it'd look great on camera, eh? In your line of work. Atmospheric. Yeah. *(Beat.)* I think its important to keep a positive attitude to things. Man should have a project. Keep him focused.

RAY: What d'you mean?

CON: Well, a friend of mine, this bloke... he says you should examine past errors. Y'know, make amends. Before you move on. That to do that you need to overcome denial and distraction. That you need to acknowledge a higher –

RAY: Sounds a bit evangelical, mate.

CON: Well, if you're not even gonna take it serious...

RAY: No, go on.

CON: Well, it's all about keeping things on track. As I say, staying focused.

RAY: What friend?

CON: Hmm?

RAY: You said a friend.

CON: Just this bloke I know.

He takes a faded blue and white rosette out of a box with a flourish.
Displays it, waiting for acknowledgement.

Fifth round cup tie. Leicester. *(Throwing the rosette to RAY, who misses it clumsily.)* Ruddock floats one in from the touchline, Sheringham takes it on his chest, traps it, turns, and spots Lovell tearing down the right wing, into the box. He gives this neat little chip over the sweeper, and I remember, I turned round to you for a second, and I swear, I can still see your grinning face, your little face grinning down at me when –

RAY: Not me.

CON: I turned back and –

RAY: Weren't me, mate.

CON: What? Yeah. Resplendent in your Farrahs. You woulda been about… sixteen.

RAY: Must've been one of your mates, Con.

CON: Down the Den. George Graham's golden season.

RAY: Nah.

CON: Fifth round cup tie. Leicester. The three of us.

RAY: Weren't me.

CON: Course it was you.

RAY: You're confusing me with someone else, Con.

CON: What're you talking about? Fifth round cup tie, Sheringham chipped it in, Lovell took it on the half volley, drove it into the top right hand corner of the net. You'd spilt brown sauce all down your Segio Tacchini.

RAY shakes his head slowly.

But I can see it, clear as day. You was clutching the hot dog in your sweaty little hand and the brown sauce –

RAY: Weren't me, Con. I never went. You're mistaken.

CON: Course it was you.

RAY: No.

CON: Fashanu came on in the second half to –

RAY: What you talking about? Fashanu never came on in the second half. And Ruddock didn't float one in to Sheringham, it was Otulakowski. Ruddock weren't even…

They stare at each other. Beat. They burst out laughing. CON turns and starts rooting through a box. RAY watches him.

CON: *(To himself.)* Got the programme here somewhere.

RAY: Don't… just don't get sucked back into all this, Con.

CON: All what?

RAY: His world.

CON: His…? I'm just going through his stuff, Ray.

RAY: I know.

CON: The man's just died.

RAY: You're grieving. I understand that. So do what you need to do. But then let it go. It's gone. His world has gone.

CON: Don't tell me *how* to do it, Ray. Don't tell me *how* to mourn the man.

RAY: I wasn't, I just meant –

CON: Because you were always trying to tell me how to –

RAY: The man weren't a legend, alright? Except in his own mind. Let's get that straight from the off.

CON: Well, thanks for that, Ray…

RAY: All I'm saying –

CON: It's great that you can swing by and distribute these little pearls of wisdom, Ray. Really, I don't know how we managed all this time without your –

RAY: I'm just saying. You've got your own family now.

CON: What?

RAY: I don't know what he did in here, and it doesn't really matter. Peggy... emailed me.

CON: Emailed you? So you have been picking up your –

RAY: No, this was about a week ago. About this studio space. And I think –

CON: Oh, Christ...

RAY: No, I think it's a good idea. Really, it's... I didn't email her back because I knew I'd be over. And I wanted to talk to you about it. Both of you. Face to face.

CON: Yeah? Well. I don't want to talk about it, Ray. There's more important –

RAY: Just... just hear me out...

CON: I can't believe she... Anyway, this isn't about *that*, Ray.

RAY: What I'm proposing is a joint venture for the –

CON: What *you're* proposing? It's not *about* you, Ray.

RAY: Excuse me?

CON: For once, it's not about you. New ventures. Fucking hell. Carving up deals on the man's coffin lid? Maybe turn his ashes into a little fucken egg timer whilst you're at it?

RAY: Okay, what's it about then, Con?

CON: This place. I wanted to show you what he did in here. I deluded myself that you might be interested.

RAY: *(Taking an envelope from his case, going to him.)* Look, Peggy explained about this little jewellery workshop she wants to set up. I think it's a cracking idea. Remember those costumes she used to do for me, when I was starting out? Those mad jackets with those fantastic little sequins? What she didn't know about polyester and bri-nylon fabrics wasn't worth knowing. I know designers out there that don't have a tenth of her –

CON: What are you, her careers adviser all of a sudden?

RAY: I'm talking about your future, Con.

CON: Oh fuck that. I don't need that from you. I'm trying to show you something here, something real. You come in here and –

RAY: Thank you. Thanks for that.

CON: For what?

RAY: Clarifying. *(He puts the envelope back into the case. Beat.)* My last interview overran. I thought I'd have more time. I should probably –

CON: Wait. At least until Peggy gets here.

RAY: I'd really like to, Con, but –

CON: He'll be here soon.

RAY: Who?

CON: Anthony. The kid I was telling you about, the one he brought here. I want you to meet him. This is what I wanted to tell you. The old man brought him here to… this is why I –

RAY: Whoa whoa whoa. When? When did the old man –

CON: About… two years ago. And I couldn't, at first, figure out why he did that, what was going through his mind. *(He is looking at the cab.)* He'd get that thousand yard stare: 'They'll fucken bury me in that.'

RAY: It was a figure of speech.

CON: Remember him saying that?

RAY: It was a figure of speech, Con.

CON: From the start, and I've been thinking about this since the funeral, I think he saw the cab as a place where he could forget who he was, where he could forget everything. It was literally like he buried himself alive in it.

RAY: You know what, Con, you should be writing the books, mate, not me. I couldn't make that shit up.

CON: You see, I think he was settling up.

RAY: Settling up what?

CON: Everything. His 'account'.

RAY: The old man killed himself, Con. That's what he did. There's no mystery here. *(Pointing at cab.)* Oh, and then he just conveniently climbed into his four wheeled coffin, like? 'Yes, guv… where to? Oh, didn't recognise you there for a second, Mr. Reaper. How's business…?'

CON: But that's how Hawkins found him.

RAY: So, if you're gonna do it you choose someplace tucked away, someplace you won't get disturbed. I'll give him credit for that. So he brought some kid here for a bit, so what? Some Billy-No-Mates he could pour whiskey and stories into. Like he'd round up all the pond life from the pub, remember? They made him feel like someone.

CON: No, Ray, he taught him.

RAY: Taught him what? Yoga? Origami?

CON: I'm serious, Ray.

RAY: Alright. Whatever you say. Whatever story you need to tell yourself, Con. Whatever gets you through. That's cool. I understand.

CON: Don't patronise me.

RAY: I wasn't. But I don't understand why you're dragging round this guilt, because –

CON: Guilt?

RAY: You did what you could, Con. No one blames you.

CON: He loved you.

RAY: Loved me? Oh yeah, he loved me with a *vengeance*.

CON: He just couldn't show it.

RAY: He was an emotional pygmy!

CON: I know he was a little rough on you, but that's –

RAY: You're a dreamer, Con, you always were. You don't remember.

CON: Why? Cos I won't allow you to remember it for me in a book, in a story?

RAY: I just meant it was different for you.

CON: How was it different?

RAY: It just was.

CON: He was the same man.

RAY: You had a toothy grin and a lovely way about you. I had shifty eyes and a centre parting. I would have voted me off the show too.

CON: A man is more than the worse thing he's ever done.

RAY: Who said that, Harold Shipman?

CON: It's all he had, Ray. On him. It's the only thing he carried. That photo of you as a kid. Not me. Not mum. You.

RAY: It's like a crap episode of Columbo, this.

CON: He carried that around. That means some –

RAY: *(Holding the photo up.)* And what's this, Con? On the back? What's this number?

CON: What? That's just…

RAY: *(As 'Columbo'.)* Er, sir, I'm sorry, just one more thing… would this be the number of this Anthony kid you keep talking about? *(Beat.)* That's why he kept it, Con. The kid's number. That's all. Had fuck all to do with me. It weren't a memento. He had the kid's number written on the back. And you phoned it, didn't you? It's a paper trail, Con.

CON: What?

RAY: Why that? Why'd they just find that photo?

CON: They found it by accident.

RAY: Nah, he was too crafty for that, too careful. He wouldn't have overlooked the details.

CON: What're you saying?

RAY: Why was there no wallet, no ID?

CON: Then what, Ray?

RAY: He did it to *punish* you, you melt.

CON: Punish me? For what?

RAY: Who knows? But there was always something. And he's still doing it, isn't he? 'Vlad The Inhaler, the asthmatic overlord of the undead.' *(Beat.)* I never told you why I quit doing stand-up, did I?

CON: You still use the name.

RAY: I'd put ten years into building that name. It was mine. I fucken *owned* it, and no fucker was gonna take that. No, I remember I gave a couple of interviews around that time. Said I was evolving. That I'd outgrown stand-up. And that what they were witnessing was the spiritual rebirth of Ray Suede. I'd taken Ray Suede the onstage persona as far as I could, that Ray Suede needed to reinvent himself as tragicomic engineer of the imagination. Some bollocks like that. But what it was, Con, I gave it up because I was shit scared. I literally could no longer stand up in a room full of people and do that stuff anymore. And it weren't stage fright. This was something else. This was real fear. Real, uncut, straight-up fear. That proper, physical, scrotum tightening fear. The kind that paralyses. Ever had that spaced out sensation when you feel your body doesn't even belong to you? Like it's just on loan? I'd been like that all afternoon before the gig. And usually, I'd clear the dressing room about an hour before and I'd kinda zone out. Y'know, I'd become Ray Suede. I'd assume the mantle. The smart casual leisurewear. The inch thick glasses. The sovereign. The lollipop. The habiliments of war. I'd just empty my mind. I'd sit there and just let 'me' drain out. I'd just let it go. And then this energy would come. From the floorboards. Honestly, I'd feel it, coming up from the fucken floorboards. And I'd just sit there and wait to be Ray Suede, just let this... this electric, kinetic, violent, hard, unyielding voice come. And it would. Always it would, if I waited, if I was patient. If I just sat and listened and waited, it'd come. But I couldn't force it. I could never force it, but it was there, if I listened hard enough. And whilst I was waiting for this to happen, for some reason (and my manager knew not to disturb me before a show), for some reason they put this call through. Someone at St. Thomas' hospital managed to get hold of his number. Could he speak to Mr. Ray Sweeney please, it was urgent. It was you. And I had, I remember this, I had the mobile in my hand and I was just staring at it. And I was... its gonna sound strange this, and you couldn't possibly have known the phone was in my hand, but I was staring at it and I was thinking: who's Ray Sweeney? Y'know? Who is that? It must've been about thirty seconds, no more than that, but it seemed like hours. And I had to... I had to will these pictures of me. I had to sit there and conjure up images of who that was. Of Ray Sweeney, this little boy I used to know. Of his mum, sat in the chair in the kitchen. Of the bedroom he shared with his little brother in Camberwell, posters of Ian Curtis on the wall. Of his Dad, standing over him. I had to think about who they were talking about til I got that picture. And your voice, in my hand, your voice was saying something about Mum, about how she's just had a stroke, and you're all waiting there at the hospital and could I come there straight after the show. And when they called me up to go on I wasn't upset about that, I wasn't thinking about Mum. I just had this picture of little Ray Sweeney in my mind. So, next thing I know, I'm on, and I'm going through my routine but I couldn't just... I didn't have the necessary distance, y'know? To do my stuff. To become Ray Suede. Cos I hadn't walked out there as Ray Suede, you see? I'd walked out as Ray Sweeney. And the stuff I was saying was… normally I'd glide through it. But this schtick I did… suddenly wasn't schtick. And suddenly I wasn't Ray Suede talking about this clueless, unlovely six-year-old who'd pissed the bed again, and getting people to laugh about it. I *was* the clueless, unlovely six-year-old boy again. With my pyjamas stuck to my legs. The light, the spotlight, in my eyes… something about the… And suddenly he was… he was standing in front of me. The door was opened and he was… the light was behind him, he was silhouetted against the… And then I could… I could hear his voice. When he opened the door, the light, behind him the… That tone he had. Clear as a bell. Low, but clear. Asking me, in that low, slow, pisstaking voice: Is that all you got, Ray? Is that all you got? And smiling, benignly, cos it was. And for a split second I was back there. He reached down the years and I felt his hand round my throat. Gently, ever so gently. Felt my spine shrink up like a question mark again as I blinked in the spotlight. He could still do that. I musta sleepwalked through the rest of the act and crept off stage. I don't even remember. But I knew then I was through.

CON: You never said. You never told me –

RAY: Stick a fork in his arse and turn him over, he's done.

The street door slams. PEGGY comes in, leading ANTHONY. He is sweating and unsteady on his feet, and leans heavily on her. CON goes over to help. RAY brings the chair over.

RAY: Here.

They sit ANTHONY down.

PEGGY: Found him up Redcross Way, near the shrine. He was sat on the pavement, nearly walked straight past him.

CON: Has he… ? *(Mimes drinking.)*

PEGGY: Didn't smell it off him.

CON: Anthony, can you tell us –

PEGGY: Should we loosen his clothes?

CON: What for?

PEGGY: He's sweating.

CON: Is he hot?

PEGGY: No, but I thought…

CON: You thought you'd just undress him.

PEGGY: You can be such an arsehole, Con.

CON: *(Slowly, to ANTHONY.)* Would you like us to phone anyone for you, Anthony? Would you like us to –

RAY: He's hypo.

CON: What?

RAY: Hypoglycaemic. The bracelet. He's wearing a… Is there a shop nearby?

PEGGY: Should we put him in the recovery –

RAY: Is there a shop? Peg! A shop. Close by.

PEGGY: Erm… on the corner. There's a –

RAY: *(Taking a fiver from his wallet.)* Get a pint of milk, some digestives and a banana.

CON: That can wait, Ray. This man could be seriously –

RAY: It's for him, you tit. *(To ANTHONY.)* How long is it since you've eaten? When did you last have something to eat?

ANTHONY looks at him. He shakes his head weakly.

RAY: Peggy.

PEGGY: *(Standing.)* Right. Yes.

She goes. The street door slams.

RAY: He just needs to get some sugars into his bloodstream. Glass of milk, a –

PEGGY comes back in.

PEGGY: It doesn't matter does it if it's chocolate Hobnobs or –

RAY: Peggy!

She goes. RAY kneels down to talk to ANTHONY.

It's okay… *(To CON.)* Anthony, was it?

CON: Yeah.

RAY: Anthony, she's just gone to get you some biscuits and milk. Is there anyone you'd like us to call?

He shakes his head no.

Alright. She won't be a sec. Alright?

ANTHONY nods.

ANTHONY: My mouth's all…

RAY: Just sit there, just relax.

CON: *(To ANTHONY.)* Got your Green Badge then?

RAY: Don't crowd him.

CON: I'm not crowding him.

RAY: Just give him a bit of –

CON: You're crowding him. *(To ANTHONY.)* Good feeling, ennit? Knight Of The Road.

RAY: Just move back a bit. He's confused, he's –

CON: 'Oh, don't crowd him, Ray.' *(To ANTHONY.)* Freedom Of The City, yeah? What, five months now? You've been qualified?

ANTHONY nods weakly.

RAY: *(Realising.)* This is the kid you… ?

CON: In here. With that map. *(Nodding at cab.)* In that… that heap of shit. *(To ANTHONY.)* Still, least you got to do most of it indoors, yeah? Nice and dry. In the flight simulator. When I was doing the knowledge I got lumbago, shooting pains all down my arm. Frozen shoulder, writer's cramp, tennis elbow, you name it. Hours I'd be out on that moped, in the rain.

RAY: What're you talking about, Con?

CON: Tell him what you told me, Anthony.

ANTHONY: My mouth's all…

RAY: He can't talk, his mouth's numb from the –

ANTHONY: Mr. Hawkins said I could take something. From the room. Keepsake.

CON: Hawkins told you that?

ANTHONY: Before he cleared… something small.

CON: Tell him what you –

ANTHONY: Good bloke. Your old man. He was a –

CON: Yeah, good bloke. That's right. Tell him what you did here, Anthony. What you told me on the phone. What you told me over –

ANTHONY falls off the chair. They help him up on to it.

ANTHONY: Yeah. In here. The old man, he…

RAY: The old man what?

ANTHONY: The map. Blue book. Knowledge.

RAY: Blue book? *(To RAY.)* What's he –

CON: In here, Ray. Taught him. In here. Not out there, not on the road. Taught him to be a cabbie. Over eighteen months. Took me three years to get my badge. Eighteen months, Ray. Imagine.

RAY: Why? Why would he –

ANTHONY falls off his chair again. PEGGY comes in with a small carrier bag.

PEGGY: What did you do to him?

CON: Nothing. He just…

She goes to help ANTHONY up. RAY assists. She takes the milk out. RAY takes the milk and opens it. He tilts ANTHONY's head back slightly and brings it to his mouth. ANTHONY drinks. Some milk runs down the side of his mouth. RAY takes the milk away. He repeats the process. He nods to the packet of biscuits. PEGGY opens them, takes one out and hands it to ANTHONY. He eats.

RAY: Alright?

ANTHONY: Sorry 'bout that.

RAY: Don't worry about it. *(To PEGGY.)* Is there anyplace he can lie down?

ANTHONY: *(Standing unsteadily.)* Nah, I'm alright. *(He sits down again.)*

PEGGY: Mick had an old camp bed out the back.

RAY: *(Nodding towards the door at the back.)* Through there?

PEGGY: It's a bit manky though.

ANTHONY: I'll be… if I can just sit here for a…

RAY: Just 'til you get your legs back.

ANTHONY: I'm fine. Don't worry. *(He stands.)* Had me milk and biscuits. *(He sits.)* Yeah. Maybe I will, just for a…

CON is staring at ANTHONY, smiling. PEGGY goes to RAY, smiling at the situation, they embrace.

RAY: *(To PEGGY.)* My timing's awful. By the time I get to Paddington –

CON: Know how they met? Discovered the kid in his flat.

RAY: Discovered?

CON: Found him turning the place over. No, it gets better. *(He is nodding at ANTHONY, encouraging him to take over the story. ANTHONY stares at him. Nodding, grinning, staring at ANTHONY.)* Lairy nineteen-year-old versus an arthritic old man. *(To ANTHONY.)* Anthony here gives him a clump, the old boy catches his head on the mantelpiece on the way down. Scarpers. *(To ANTHONY.)* Yeah? So, he's out cold on the carpet, and he gets this clot. But Anthony here… Anthony thinks he might've killed him. Gets twitchy. Puts in an anonymous call. Weren't too clever covering his self, so they pull him in. Turns out, that call saved Mick's life. So: robbery with aggravated assault. Twelve months, does six. So *then* the old man decides to visit him, cos he can't work out why the kid made the call in the first place, and why he didn't keep schtum. Becomes his pen pal, for fuck's sake.

RAY: Pen pal?

CON: So when he gets out, the old man tells him about this place. Says he'll teach him.

ANTHONY: *(Lurching to his feet.)* Think I'm gonna be sick.

RAY goes to him.

CON: *(Nods towards the door at the back.)* On the left.

RAY helps ANTHONY out the back.

PEGGY: *(Sotto.)* Did you ask him?

CON: *(Sotto.)* Jesus Christ, Peg…

PEGGY: *(Sotto.)* What we talked about –

CON: *(Sotto.)* It's like Piccadilly Circus in here. I can't talk to him about it when the kid's just –

PEGGY: *(Sotto.)* So you *did* ask him?

CON: *(Sotto.)* I'm just starting to get through to him. Can't you see that? I think he's actually coming round to the idea of filming in here.

PEGGY: *(Sotto.)* Filming?

CON: *(Sotto.)* Yeah. A kind of epilogue, a valediction for –

PEGGY: *(Sotto.)* But you did *ask* him?

CON: *(Sotto.)* I… yes. A new sequence for the TV show. Says he'll speak to his people about it.

PEGGY: *(Sotto.)* Really?

CON: *(Sotto.)* Yeah, he's… ask him what?

PEGGY: *(Sotto.)* About the money. *(CON just stares at her. Sotto.)* And?

CON: *(Sotto.)* He'll... think about it.

PEGGY: *(Sotto.)* Think about what?

CON: *(Sotto.)* He'll...

PEGGY: *(Sotto.)* He said yes, didn't he?

CON: *(Sotto.)* I... he said...

PEGGY: *(Sotto.)* I can't believe it. *(She kisses him.)* And for the full amount? For the –

CON: *(Sotto.)* Listen, Peg...

PEGGY: *(Sotto.)* I'll talk to the woman, I've got her card in my... we could arrange a viewing tonight. After. We can get a stud partition to –

CON: *(Sotto.)* Peg...

PEGGY: *(Sotto.)* We'll divide the studio. I could use my old college tools to start off, a small workbench, a vice, some –

CON: *(Sotto.)* I didn't actually... when the kid came in... before I...

Beat. She stares at him.

PEGGY: *(Sotto.)* You didn't ask.

CON: *(Sotto.)* I was gonna. I swear. As soon as I –

PEGGY: *(Sotto.)* You spineless imbecile.

CON: *(Sotto.)* Listen, the minute I get him on his –

PEGGY: *(Sotto.)* You know what it's like living with you, Con? It's like having a wank with a withered arm.

The toilet flushes, off.

PEGGY: *(Sotto.)* Ask him. Don't let him –

RAY enters. PEGGY takes the milk and biscuits from the table.

PEGGY: *(To RAY, exiting out back.)* Just in case.

CON: *(Indicating room, expansively.)* Well, what d'you think? This place.

RAY: For… ?

CON: What we were talking about.

RAY: The workshop?

CON: *(Lost in his world.)* Perfect, ennit?

RAY: This near the river? That's a tidy few quid, Con.

CON: Great location.

RAY: You got the freehold on it? You mentioned a landlord.

CON: Might want to hang a few lights in here though. Bit gloomy.

RAY: What're you talking about, Con? I thought we were talking about –

CON: Your TV show. I've been thinking about it. This place. An epilogue, whatever you call it. I know you woulda shot most of it by now, but –

RAY: An epilogue.

CON: It's too late for the book, obviously, that's already out, but I thought you could talk to them about this place.

RAY: Sorry, who?

CON: Your producers. About filming in here. With the kid. The map. The knowledge. First time I saw this place it hit me like a bolt of lightning: your book. The stories. Cos I was thinking: he was a storyteller, yeah? He was like you like that.

RAY: He weren't like me, Con…

CON: I couldn't write it down, though, you'd need to do all that. Remember he used to tell those stories, coming up from Auntie Jeannie's, in the cab? Like he'd just… weave them out of the night or something…

RAY: What d'you mean he was like me?

43

CON: So, the sequence starts off… I'm five years old, I'm sat up front in the cab, and I'm asking him: Dad, how'd you get that scar on your cheek? 'Member that scar he had?

RAY: *(To himself.)* Oh, Christ…

CON: 'Well, now, me and Cuchulain was back to back, fighting these English giants outside the Gin Palace on the Old Kent road one time and this giant blindsided me and glassed me from behind, when I was off balance like…'

RAY: *(Smiling.)* Fuck sake, Con…

CON: Then, right, then you do a dissolve from me as a boy, in the cab, poodling along, five years old, listening to all this, wide eyed, to the cab, here – now – in this room, except now it's Anthony who's –

RAY: Cuchulainn?

CON: Yeah, I know. I was five. I was like 'Giants… on the Old Kent road… Fuck!' Y'know?

RAY: I don't believe this.

CON: And I understand why you wrote what you wrote about him. To an extent. Because you weren't in full possession of all the facts. I understand that. Here's our chance to bring it all –

RAY: I told you, the book is a comic fantasia… it's not even *about* that. For a start it's a work of fiction, and secondly –

CON: Peggy might have her fanny in a knot about the book, but personally I don't give a shit… but the old man? Dragging his name through the mud, it's not –

RAY: You know how he got that scar, Con?

CON: Yeah. Course.

RAY: I mean, how he *really* got it.

CON: Yeah.

RAY: And it weren't fighting English giants with Cuchulainn.

CON: I'm not fucking thick, Ray.

RAY: I didn't say you were thick.

CON: I know Cuchulainn weren't a real bloke.

RAY: He got that scar when he –

CON: It's an Irish myth, ennit? The point is –

RAY: He destroyed my life, Con.

CON: So what is it, revenge?

RAY: It's my story.

CON: All I'm saying… *(Suddenly remembering.)* Shit. What time is it?

RAY: Yeah. *(Glances at watch.)* I need to be –

CON: I have to feed the metre. You alright for a few minutes?

RAY: Con, I have to –

CON: Won't be a sec. *(Exiting.)* Think about what I said.

He goes.

RAY listens for the street door to slam. When it does he slowly turns around and looks at the room, as if properly, for the first time, taking in the damp, joyless atmosphere, imagining.

He looks a long while at the cab. Remembering, he takes an envelope from his jacket and slips it into PEGGY's bag. He takes his jacket off and hangs it on a nail in the wall, next to the plaid jacket.

There is a brief rustling noise, somewhere from the back of the lock up. He freezes, alert, tense. He listens. Silence.

The rustling noise again. This time he hears it more distinctly. It comes from one of the cardboard boxes lining the back wall. He moves towards them and stops before them, listening intently.

Another, smaller rustle. He crouches to a box on the floor, at the back. Cautiously, with infinite slowness, he opens the box. A pigeon bursts out from it, thrashing its wings violently and swooping up to the rafters, where it thrashes about before it eventually settles.

RAY, very startled, stands there breathing hard, trying to catch his breath. He brushes himself down. He stoops slightly, and hunches his shoulders, then looks up and stares at the bird.

RAY: *(To the rafters, in a thick aggressive Westmeath accent, sotto voce.)* You'll not best me, yer feathered cunt.

Brief tableaux. Slow fade to black.

ACT TWO

RAY and PEGGY. Half an hour later. PEGGY sits watching him attentively.

RAY is playing a small, tinny, Casiotone keyboard. Or rather, he is holding it up as it plays a pre-programmed, simplistic melody and rhythm. He half sings, half proclaims his song, Farewell, England's Mongrel Breed *in a style that is a bastard hybrid of Rex Harrison and Mark E. Smith:*

England belongs to me, and
My England belongs to the world of never will be, so
Farewell, England's mongrel breed:
Farewell, Phil Larkin rotting away in a library in Hull.
Farewell, stewed tea. Bad teeth.
And Barry Foster's grin in *Frenzy.*

Farewell, the cramped joy of paddling pools full of idiot children
Seen from a South West train
Rolling over the small back gardens,
The mini-Edens, of Hersham.
Farewell, Jarvis Cocker. And sentimental gangsters.
And Murco garages. And Ginster's pasties.

Farewell, Michael Powell in exile after *Peeping Tom.*
Farewell, Morrissey on Top Of The Pops.
And the number 8 routemaster bus.
And Frazzles from vending machines.
And pissing in the chlorine at the Lido.
Farewell, discarded copies of Razzler in surburban hedgerows.

And did those feet, in ancient times
Wear Converse trainers
And walk upon cracked paving slabs on Camberwell Green?
And would the holy countenance divine
Spit from my stereo rhymes sublime
As my Chariot of Fire gets snarled up
Round the Catford gyratory system and red lights?

Farewell, Joanna Lumley in The Avengers, and Mark E. Smith.
And *The Great Escape* on telly at Christmas.
And doing cross-country runs in the rain in your plimsols.
Half day closing. Jumble sales. Ancient Lights.
Farewell, a general sense of apathy and paralysis.
And my uncle Joe puking up his false teeth at Christmas when pissed.

But before you sink, finally, beneath toxic waves of roiling seas,
Rise up once more, England's mongrel breed,
Out of the ashes of cheap nostalgia shows, I summon thee
And crest the waves on an armada of rusting supermarket trolleys
Down Thames estuary.
And save us from this great floating turd of carcinogenic dreams,
And corporate sponsorship, and dead memory,
And the plastic stink of Starbucks coffee.
And polystyrene cups spilling builders tea.

I will not cease from mental fight
Nor shall the sword sleep in my hand
'Til I have slain the last blue & yellow dragon
Of flat pack assembly furniture & meatballs Scandinavian
I will not cease from mental fight
I will not cease from mental fight…

He turns off the Casiotone keyboard. PEGGY, delighted, claps.

RAY: There's another eighteen verses, but you get the drift.

PEGGY: The gift that keeps on giving.

RAY: I offered it to HBO as the theme song for the show, but they thought it wouldn't, er, 'resonate' with their target demographic.

PEGGY: Feed the metre. Fucken idiot. I told him I put it in the car park.

RAY: *(Laughs.)* He's looking well.

PEGGY: Not as well as you.

RAY: Well, he was always a fat bastard so I suppose the difference is more noticeable with him.

PEGGY: He adores you, Ray. He does. He idolises you.

RAY: Con's not the adoring type.

PEGGY: It's good he got to see you. Four years, eh? Where does it go? What did you talk about? Anything in particular?

RAY: Oh, this and that. *(Beat.)* I always… Don't take this the wrong way, but I always thought it was a bit weird how you two ended up together. You always seemed to have more… well, drive.

PEGGY: It's not drive he lacks, Ray, its focus. I don't know anyone who works harder, or for longer, with so little to show for it.

RAY: It's not all it's cracked up to be. So-called success.

PEGGY: Sure.

RAY: Success on that very shallow, superficial –

PEGGY: When do we get what's ours, Ray? That's all I want to know.

RAY: How d'you mean?

PEGGY: When do we get what we deserve, what we've earnt? What's his by rights. When does that start to kick in?

RAY: What is his by rights?

PEGGY: I didn't mean… its a figure of speech, I just meant –

RAY: It wasn't a figure of speech, Peggy. What has he earned? That's been denied him?

PEGGY: Come on, Ray…

RAY: My book?

PEGGY: You know what's what. Don't make out you don't know what's what.

RAY: My book, you mean?

PEGGY: You don't think he's a bit entitled?

RAY: Entitled to what?

PEGGY: Come on, Ray…

RAY: A percentage of net sales? Royalties? Co-authorship, what?

PEGGY: You want me to spell it out?

RAY: I wrote it, Peggy, all by myself, that's how it works, if you write some –

PEGGY: It's him. The character in the book, the idiot savant visionary loser, the daydreamer, it's Con.

RAY: No it isn't. Not directly. It's a –

PEGGY: Don't tell me it's an amalgam of different personalities you met on the stand-up circuit, don't you dare give me that shit. And it hurt. He won't say, but it hurt. He may act like an idiot, when it suits him, but he's not. Not really.

RAY: I never said Con was an idiot.

PEGGY: No, you don't say it.

RAY: It might be true I've endowed the character with many of the qualities that Con himself –

PEGGY: This is me you're talking to now, Ray.

RAY: Anyway, is it so unflattering? They're qualities I myself wished I had, tenacity and –

PEGGY: Save it for the celebrity love-in, Ray. You've compressed all the worst qualities of his personality, the creeping, wasting, daydreaming nothing that his life has become, and –

RAY: You sure you're talking about what *I've* done now? *(He notices she is on the verge of tears, goes to her.)* Hey…

She moves away.

PEGGY: Don't. Don't be nice to me, Ray…

RAY: What is it?

PEGGY: Nothing. It's stupid.

RAY: Hey, come on, Peg…

PEGGY: That thing you were singing. About old feet and Converse trainers. *(She inhales deeply, takes a moment.)* Heather came home, couple of days ago, and she was so… she's eight, and she just got really upset, I'd bought these Converse trainers for her birthday, but I was short last week so I… and she came back and she said how she had told all her friends she was going to get these… and I bought her these quite cheap copies from the market, and she said her friends said they were 'snide' and she…

RAY: Converse?

PEGGY: *(Looking at him sharply.)* What?

RAY: Converse, you say?

PEGGY: Why?

RAY: What size is she? We could –

PEGGY: You can be such an arsehole, Ray.

RAY: No, I just mean, it wouldn't be obvious that I'd –

PEGGY: Just… don't, okay? Just…

RAY: It would be a loan, you can –

PEGGY: It's not about the fucking trainers, Ray!

RAY: Oh.

PEGGY: Con's working as an assistant warehouse supervisor at the Croydon IKEA. I mean, I should be thankful he's got a job at all. Things have been…

RAY: He never said.

PEGGY: What's he gonna say? 'I'm assistant warehouse supervisor at the Croydon IKEA?' 'Oh, and by the way, I lost my licence, and the Public Carriages Office barred me from ever carrying one again?' Bit of a conversation killer, ennit?

RAY: His cab licence? They can't do that.

PEGGY: Well, apparently, if you mount the pavement at Finsbury Circus at two in the afternoon, with passengers on board they can.

RAY: What, did he blackout?

PEGGY: He was drunk. The only good thing was he didn't manage to maim or kill anyone. He just missed driving through the plate glass window of Pizza Express.

RAY: But why didn't he tell me?

PEGGY: He's hardly gonna boast about it, is he?

RAY: How long have things been like this?

PEGGY: About two years.

RAY: Two years?

PEGGY: We'd been saving up. We were looking at setting up a restaurant.

RAY: Really?

PEGGY: Well, more of a small bistro, to start off. I say Bistro. I suppose I'm talking about a take away caff to kick off. Bacon butties and Lattes. Build it up from there. I sent you an email but you obviously never got it.

RAY: No, I got it. And I was gonna talk to you actually about –

PEGGY: Con's a fantastic cook. I mean, really.

RAY: You see, I never knew that.

PEGGY: Well, you've been away. And even before that you weren't around much. Really, he's very good. He took a night class a few years back. It's a passion of his. He'd go round to friends' houses and cook for them, and then he started to get a reputation, y'know, there was such good word of mouth. So then he started doing it for a bit of money on the side. Not much more than expenses at first really, but it was great experience for him. And he loved it. He'd come home and he'd be absolutely wiped, but you could see how happy it made him. He was like a kid. But that's Con. Like a kid who wants to please everyone all of the time.

RAY: So what does he cook?

PEGGY: South East Asian and Mediterranean fusion. Mainly Thai and southern Italy. No, don't laugh, really, it's very good. We've even had these food snobs round and when we told them what it was they raised one weary eyebrow, but when they tasted it...

RAY: Yeah?

PEGGY: We'd started to host these small dinner parties. They became, well, I'm bigging it up now, but really, Ray, it's no exaggeration to say they were kinda legendary around Lewisham.

RAY: That's great. I never knew.

PEGGY: Well, there's a few things you don't know about us.

RAY: I'm sure there is.

PEGGY: We're not quite the cartoon troglodytes we're sometimes painted.

RAY: Oh. We're back to the book.

PEGGY: Yeah, Ray, the book.

RAY: I told you, Peg. It's not him. It's not you.

PEGGY: But people think it is.

RAY: Then they're idiots. What people?

PEGGY: They'd come round, after seeing you on the telly, or hearing you on the radio, and they'd do these crap impersonations. They'd do these little routines they'd seen you do, messing up all of the punchlines, y'know, your character 'Charlie'...

RAY: And that's all he is, a character, a composite –

PEGGY: The daydreaming south London, second generation paddy taxi driver, who drives his black cab in a homicidal rage, fantasising about the different ways he can kill his redheaded harridan of a wife...

RAY: So I drew on elements of my own upbringing, but it's fiction, Peg, fiction.

PEGGY: Except they weren't really doing impersonations of you doing your character, they were impersonating Con. At our dinner party. In our home. Where we were hosts. Where Con was serving his southeast Asian-Mediterranean fusion cuisine, they were 'doing' him. And he would serve the food and grin like an idiot, and take it all in good part. But I could see he was dying inside. And they'd ask him: 'But Con, mate, why hasn't he "done" your fusion cuisine, why hasn't he put that in the book', and Con would patiently explain that the character in the book wasn't actually him, it was an amalgam of... but they kept on and on asking him why? Why? Until I turned to them, grinning like a Rottweiler, and said: 'Because he doesn't know every fucking thing about us, you thick cunt.' Well, as you can imagine, that was the end of the south east Asian-Mediterranean fusion cuisine dinner parties. And he didn't say. Con. He never said anything.

RAY: Can't he appeal it? Surely they've –

PEGGY: He's an alcoholic, Ray. *(Beat.)* He's been clean and sober now about eighteen months. But we ate into all our savings. There was a civil law suit from the passenger he nearly killed... actually she just got a broken collar bone, but you know what those ambulance chasers are like. We had twenty grand put aside. With the business enterprise initiative, some loans... sixty, seventy grand, start-up costs.

RAY: But your end was twenty?

PEGGY: Yeah. We've got a couple of things lined up. We'll be alright. *(Upbeat.)* But what about you, Ray? How are things with you? How's the tour going?

RAY: Okay.

PEGGY: Sounds exciting. Varied.

RAY: You get shunted about a bit on these trips, y'know? Logistically it's…

PEGGY: I can imagine.

RAY: Two days in Rotterdam, a morning in Seville, a night in Edinburgh, a day in Dublin, and four days in London with a whole day off yesterday factored into the…

Beat.

PEGGY: Go on.

RAY: *(Laughs.)* Listen to me.

PEGGY: Yesterday?

RAY: Yeah, it was very short notice.

PEGGY: You should've come round.

RAY: I know, but it really was a last minute… it wasn't even on the schedule…

PEGGY: Con would've loved that.

RAY: Me too.

PEGGY: It just seems all so rushed. This. An hour before you have to…

RAY: These trips are… it's just the airport, the car, the room, the venue, the bar, the interview, the… I spend a lot of time just looking out of plane windows. Ever noticed how from a certain height all cities at night look like raked coals on a dying fire?

PEGGY: No.

RAY: No, I… a lot of planes, as I say.

PEGGY: We were hoping to get away someplace this year. Someplace hot. That heat that gets into your bones. Proper Mediterranean heat. It'll probably be Lewisham though. Still, I hear it's lovely, this time of year. Oh, you haven't seen any recent photos of the girls, have you?

RAY: Don't think I have, no.

PEGGY: I've one of them in a kinda X-Factor type thing they did at the school. *(Goes to her bag.)* Heather's such a piss taker, you'd love her, she's got such an acid tongue. Gemma's more… *(She pulls out the envelope.)* What's this?

RAY: Ah. That was for later.

PEGGY: What is it?

RAY: Open it.

She does so. It's a cheque.

PEGGY: Ray…

RAY: It's exactly one third of what I got for the option of the first book. Forty five thou.

PEGGY: *(Peering at it.)* Oh, hold on…

RAY: Oh, I didn't put the wrong date down, did I? I'm terrible for –

PEGGY: It's made out just to me.

RAY: Yeah.

PEGGY: Suppose it doesn't matter, it's a joint –

RAY: It's yours. Just you. Not you and Con. I've got one made out to him for the same amount. His end. One third. It's ours, Peg. Cos it's our story. Who else am I gonna share it with?

PEGGY: Ray, I can't take this.

RAY: Yes you can.

PEGGY: Yes I can, actually. *(Laughs.)* Ray, you don't know what this means. But this is too much…

RAY: I got an advance for the next book. And I do know what it means, Peg. I know what it is, the book.

PEGGY: Ray, I don't think Con will –

RAY: No, he won't take his of course. He'll say it's blood money.

PEGGY: I mean he won't accept this.

RAY: Probably not.

PEGGY: So I can't take it.

RAY: Why not?

PEGGY: You know why.

RAY: Course you can. It's yours. So tell him or don't tell him.

PEGGY: How d'you mean?

RAY: I mean it's yours. Whether you keep it or not, that's different. That's your call. Split it with Con, or…

PEGGY: Or what?

RAY: You don't owe him, Peggy. Not anymore.

PEGGY: What does that mean?

RAY: You've got drive, ambition, vision…

PEGGY: What does that mean, Ray?

RAY: It's your money, Peggy. You do what you need to do, that's your call. This just gives you some options. Maybe your own studio space, some tools.

She stares at him. Looks at the cheque. She places the cheque on the table near him. She nods, to herself.

PEGGY: It's very kind of you, Ray, incredibly kind, but you know I can't accept this.

RAY: Put it in your bag, Peggy.

PEGGY: I don't think so.

RAY: Don't be silly now.

PEGGY: So, you listened to me… beg? How was that for you, Ray?

RAY: What?

PEGGY: You stood there, listened to me plead with you, all the time you got this burning a hole in your pocket.

RAY: Wasn't like that.

PEGGY: Listened to me bleating like a stuck pig, all our woes, our troubles…

RAY: It wasn't –

PEGGY: Loved all that, didn't you? Standing there with that lovely 'inner glow', standing there like fucken Bono with that smug…

RAY picks the cheque up and presses it into her hand. They are very close.

RAY: Just hold onto it for a bit, Peg. Don't have to cash it. Con doesn't have to know. I didn't know what the fuck I was gonna do with it when I came here, to be honest with you. I love him, Peg, but I can't just stand by and watch him bleed you like this. He's a good man, Peg. The best. But sometimes I think he's got too much of the old feller in him, and he's not ready to let him go. Cos I watched mum's life run through her hands like sand as he pissed her future away. And it doesn't have to be that way. You have the girls. I didn't know whether I was gonna say that, but fuck it, it's said now. I'm shaking here. So. No commitment. Just get used to the feel of it. For a bit.

The street door slams, off. A moment later CON appears.

CON: I was walking up and down Union street, walked up as far as the Borough, thought it'd been pinched, before I realised.

PEGGY: Pillock. Told you it was in the car park.

CON: How's Anthony?

PEGGY: Sleeping.

CON looks at them a moment.

PEGGY: What?

RAY: No, I was just telling Peg. When he'd take us out for a spin. *(To PEGGY.)* As I was saying, some Sundays, he'd take us down to Kent, in the cab. Let us sit up front. To

Auntie Jeannie's in Sevenoaks. On the way back he'd take different routes in. Come on, lads, he'd say, tell me the way, I'm lost. *(To CON.)* The only thing I ever remember doing with him that was any fun. Con always got it right.

CON: Not always.

RAY: Con was good like that. Good memory. I was always the daydreamer then, not him. I could never remember the street names. The old man'd call out to all these people on the way, everyone seemed to know him. I used to think there wasn't a place in London where his name wasn't known. *(To CON.)* You were always good at that, weren't you?

CON: And you always had a vivid imagination, didn't you? Teachers were always… in English, in Drama…

PEGGY: Think he's alright back there?

CON: Better look in on him.

PEGGY goes out back. Beat.

RAY: Teachers were always what, Con? You said –

CON: No, they just said you had a vivid imagination, that's all.

RAY: What does that mean?

CON: Things coming out of the wallpaper…

RAY: What're you talking about?

CON: Faces. Voices. Strange figures…

RAY: What d'you mean?

CON: Nothing. Like you said, You were… inventive.

RAY: Inventive?

CON: Yeah, you'd… I remember, in our bedroom, you'd create these little worlds. These whole worlds. Little stories.

RAY: You mean I made things up.

CON: No, just you were… artistic.

RAY: What does that mean?

CON: You know, arty.

RAY: You don't mean arty.

CON: Don't go getting all paranoid now, Ray.

RAY: What stories did I make up? That he beat me?

CON: Did I say that?

RAY: What, I embellished?

CON: I didn't say that.

RAY: Spiced it up a bit, you mean.

CON: I didn't mean it like that.

RAY: Made a big drama out of it, cos I was good at that, wasn't I? You just said.

CON: Look, I know you had a rough time with him, okay?

RAY: A rough time?

CON: I know you two never saw eye to –

RAY: He beat me up, Con. He beat me the way a man would beat another man. He punched me, flush, in the face, like he would a man.

CON: Cos you pushed his buttons…

RAY: I was a kid, Con. A boy. A child. He was a grown –

CON: But I never saw it.

Beat.

RAY: Sorry, what did you just say?

CON: I never… he never, all I'm saying is, it was always when I was out. It was always when you were… alone with him.

RAY: And what, Con?

CON: Nothing. I'm just saying.

RAY: I did it to myself? The marks, the cuts, the bruising, the broken...

CON: All I'm –

RAY: Was that all me? Did I...?

CON: I just never *saw* that side of him. I'm not saying it didn't happen, I just didn't... I never actually saw him... you say he did this and he did that, okay, maybe he did... but I didn't see it. So why didn't it happen to me?

RAY: I don't know why. Did you ever ask him?

CON: Why didn't he beat me? Why didn't he do it to me?

RAY: Because he *hid* it from you. That's why. He'd wait til you were out or had gone to bed. Except that time.

CON: Which time?

RAY: The time on the landing. At the top of the stairs.

Beat. RAY waits. CON now remembers.

RAY: Yeah. That time. The time with my little pool cue. Remember that half-size pool cue I had? When he did it in front of you. To show you.

CON: I... I don't...

RAY: You don't what?

CON: I don't remember it that way.

RAY: What way do you remember it? How could you remember it other than how it was?

CON: You were...

RAY: Go on.

CON: It was different. He snapped. You were... and I'm saying he was wrong, I'm not saying he was right, I'm saying he was totally out of... but you were goading him

RAY: Goading him?

CON: I'm not saying he was –

RAY: Goading him?

CON: Seeing how far you could... and he just snapped.
I... there was a black fire in his eyes that night. I didn't
recognise him that night, I'd never seen him like –

RAY: What didn't you recognise? Cos I recognised him straight
away.

Beat.

CON: I'm not saying he was right.

RAY: How could you remember it different to how it was?

CON: But why didn't he do it to me?

RAY: Because he loved you.

CON: He loved you too, Ray. He just couldn't... after you left
he'd always talk about you. I'd hear him. Downstairs, with
the boys, playing cards in the kitchen. How proud. What
you were doing, your stand-up. Telling his mates. And I
think... I used to listen to him and I honestly think that's
where you get it from. The storytelling. He used to say –

RAY: That lying fake bastard! He never invented me! I
invented me! I invented Ray Suede! He never invented –

CON: You're like him, more than you'll ever –

RAY: He was a locust, he just consumed everything in front of
him. He thought that's what everything was there for, for
him to eat up. But you never really *saw* him, did you?

CON: I saw him. What're you talking about? I saw him.

RAY: Not really, Con.

CON: I just didn't see him the way *you* saw him, the way you
wrote it.

RAY: This again? Look, Con –

CON: But why do *you* get to tell it?

RAY: There was nothing stopping you. There was no
injunction saying –

CON: I'm no writer, Ray. You're the writer.

RAY: What did you want, for me to erase it? For me to pretend it never –

CON: You're the storyteller. Yours is the version they accept. Yours is the –

RAY: Yes. But I don't have final say in the… I don't actually get to –

CON: You wrote it and now they're making a –

RAY: They chucked me off, Con.

CON: What?

RAY: The show. They chucked me off. Alright? Happy?

CON: Your show? How could they do that? You're the –

RAY: Cos that's how it works, Con.

CON: But it's your show. That doesn't even make –

RAY: They just optioned the book. There's no obligation for them to… the contract gives them the option to use me on the scriptwriting team, if they decide I'm up to it. As I don't have experience as a script… Look, I was working under the story editor.

CON: It's your book.

RAY: Yeah, and I was the script consultant.

CON: On your own book?

RAY: I'm no scriptwriter. That's not my forte.

CON: You didn't write the show?

RAY: I… advised on the show.

CON: Advised?

RAY: They were really encouraged by some of the story elements. Really encouraged. They just thought some of my script was… I mean, they liked loads of stuff about –

CON: Was what?

RAY: Was… well, the way they put it –

CON: Was what, Ray?

RAY: Dramatically inert.

CON: It's still the same story though, isn't it?

RAY: Yes. Mainly.

CON: Well, it is or it isn't.

RAY: Most of the elements of the –

CON: Which elements?

RAY: The core elements.

CON: Did you write any of it?

RAY: I… provided the building blocks.

CON: They changed it completely?

RAY: Not changed, exactly…

CON: What's changed?

RAY: The fundamentals are still –

CON: What did they change?

RAY: They… it's not a case of *change*, exactly, they've just culturally reconfigured –

CON: What does that mean?

RAY: They felt – and I'd have to agree with them on this, that relocating the action to Brooklyn, we –

CON: Brooklyn. Right. So what else did they change?

RAY: Nothing, in essence, really has –

CON: What else?

RAY: They thought the couple were a bit too old.

CON: Me and Peg?

RAY: I told you, it's not you and –

CON: Come on, Ray!

RAY: They felt it would have more cultural resonance over there if the Charlie character worked as a motorman on the New York subway.

CON: So he's not even a cabbie?

RAY: He's still a driver of sorts.

CON: And what about the old man? Who's playing him now, Morgan Freeman?

RAY: The essence of –

CON: What does the old man do?

RAY: He's a motorman too.

CON: Has she still got red hair?

RAY: They've kept true to the spirit of –

CON: Has she still got red hair?

RAY: Yes. They liked the red hair.

CON: Oh, they liked the red hair did they?

RAY: They just wanted, they said, the whole thing, without changing the vital elements of it, they just wanted to give it some topspin.

CON: Topspin.

RAY: They wanted to… look, I wasn't too chuffed about it either, Con. It was in the contract. It was either that or walk away and –

CON: Leave the money. Yeah, that woulda been criminal, Ray.

RAY stares at him a moment, lost for words. He looks crestfallen for a second, but suddenly bursts out laughing, shaking his head. He walks over to the plaid jacket on the hanger.

RAY: The old man woulda loved that, wouldn't he? Oh yeah. He'd have had a field day. *(He puts on the jacket.)* 'Sold yer soul, Ray. Did ye get the best price, though, Ray? Did ye sell to the highest bidder? Ye didn't go in too low, did ye?'

CON: You used to freak me out with that shit.

RAY: Remember?

CON: Standing outside the bedroom, calling into me.

RAY: It was like I was only *really* me when I was pretending to be him.

CON: That slow walk he'd have, coming up the stairs.

RAY: *(Adopts a thick Westmeath accent.)* You'll not best me, yer c-c-c-cunt. *(He sets his jaw, tilts his chin up slightly.)* I said, yer'll –

CON: But Daddy, Ray said –

RAY: Don't be squealing on Ray now, Con.

CON: Sorry, Daddy.

RAY: Cos we know what happens to squealers, don't we, Ray?

CON: They get bled.

RAY: They get strung up by their ankles and bled, that's right. And then we cut rashers from them. And the leavings is sausage meat. Are ye sausage meat, Con?

CON: No, Daddy, please, I wasn't trying to –

RAY: Stop yer fuckin yap now, Con.

CON: But Daddy, I was just –

RAY: Leave it be. And you, Ray, you've the face of what ye are, haven't ye?

CON: What's that?

RAY: A right fuckin' blaggard.

CON: No, Daddy, I don't have the face of –

RAY: Ye know what ye are, Ray?

CON: What?

RAY: Will I tell ye?

CON: No. No, don't tell me.

RAY: Will I tell ye what ye are? Yis all fart and no shit, that what ye are. Go up into the garden now, Con.

CON: Ah, no, Daddy...

RAY: Go up into the garden and cut me a stick.

CON: Ray didn't mean to –

RAY: Not too thick now, Con. Something with a bit of give in it, something with a bit of snap, like.

CON: Daddy, Ray wrote a book...

RAY: Wrote a book is it? Ah well, Ray's very smart isn' he?

CON: Isn' he?

RAY: Ray's a kinda smooth boy, isn' he?

CON: Isn't he though, Dad?

RAY: A kinda fly boy. See, Ray's very book smart, Con. Aren't ye, Ray?

CON: I don't know if I am or I'm not.

RAY: Yer a right bag of monkeys, aren't ye, Ray?

CON: Am I?

RAY: A bag of little monkeys smothered in grease.

CON: Why am I a bag of monkeys smothered in grease, Daddy?

RAY: Cos yer a slippery customer.

CON: I'm not.

RAY: Oh, but ye are.

CON: I'm not, Daddy.

RAY: Oh, but ye are, Ray. A slippy, greasy little monkey.

CON: But if you're slippy no one can catch ahold of yer, can they?

RAY: That's right, son, that's right. He has a point, Con. Being slippy's okay, Ray, if you want to be known about the town as a sneaky little shilly-shally Go-By-The-Wall, creeping round doors, sweating in company and never standing yer height.

CON: But I do stand my height, Daddy.

RAY: No, yer kinda crooked, Ray.

CON: No, look, I'm standing my height now, I'm –

RAY: Yer kinda crooked inside, Ray. Yer kinda shrivelled up. Look at me. I stand me height. And what did I land in this poxy town with? Only three pound in me pocket and a cardboard suitcase. *(He brandishes his fist.)* Mother fist and her five lovely daughters. I lived on me fuckin' wits, son.

CON: Oh, so did I, Daddy.

RAY: You? What did you do?

CON: I lived on my wits too. *(Attempting to break the game.)* Alright, Ray, come on…

RAY: Did yer now?

CON: Leave it now…

RAY: What, telling jokes, is it?

CON: I said that's enough, Ray.

RAY: How is it the same?

CON: You always have to take it too far, Ray, you always –

RAY: Standing up and telling jokes to a room full of strangers, to get them to like ye? I'm not talking about that, Ray. I'm not talking about currying favour, Ray, licking someone's hole to get them to say well done, get them to love you for half an hour like a cheap slag, I'm talking about survival. Doing what ye had to do to survive. Cos you're nothing to me, ye little fucken scrote. I could reach down your throat, pull your heart out and eat it raw in front of you and I'd still have enough room left for me steak and chips and me bottle of fucken Tizer.

CON: I said leave it!

RAY: *(Dropping the accent.)* He despised us! When're you gonna wake up to yourself?

They are face to face. ANTHONY comes out of the back room. They look at him. PEGGY follows him out.

PEGGY: He heard you shouting.

CON: Yeah. Sorry about that.

ANTHONY: I thought… from back there it sounded like… *(He is looking at RAY.)*

CON: How are you feeling?

ANTHONY: Alright. Yeah, much better, thanks.

CON: Good.

ANTHONY: *(To RAY.)* With the jacket, when I came out, the way you're standing and everything, it's…

RAY takes the jacket off and hangs it up.

RAY: We were just messing about. Got a bit carried away. Sorry about that.

ANTHONY: Thought I was goofing off back there, y'know? The voice. How he used to…

RAY: These old buildings, the acoustics…

ANTHONY: Cos that's exactly how he'd call them street names. Standing there. Like that. Barking them out. Used to shit me up.

CON: Yeah. I bet.

ANTHONY: Like being in the army or something.

CON: Yeah, he could be a bit…

ANTHONY: He was solid. Yeah? Everything around him moved, all that shit out there, it's all... y'know? All the time. Every direction. Changing. But he was...

Beat. RAY puts on his own jacket.

RAY: Know what I can't work out, Anthony? Why you weren't at the funeral.

ANTHONY: Weren't my scene.

RAY: Oh. *(To CON.)* It weren't his scene. *(To ANTHONY.)* What's your scene then, Anthony?

ANTHONY: I don't do the family thing really, y'know?

RAY: I see.

ANTHONY: Yeah. When you rang, when you mentioned you was his son and that, when you told me, I thought: Nah. Can't be getting into all that. Y'know?

PEGGY: All what?

ANTHONY: Y'know. All that.

CON: What you did in here, Anthony... we were just talking about it. Me and Ray.

ANTHONY: Oh yeah?

CON: That was pretty full on, wasn't it? Pretty hardcore.

ANTHONY: Suppose it was, yeah.

CON: What, six hours a day, five, six days a week?

ANTHONY: Sometimes, yeah.

CON: It's impressive. No, really, it is. We were just saying. As a young man, as a twenty year old, I don't think I –

ANTHONY: Nineteen.

CON: What?

ANTHONY: I was nineteen.

CON: Well, there you go. I wouldn't have had the discipline.

ANTHONY: He was... straight down the line. Your old man. Hard. Could handle himself. Mentally, as well. All the stuff he, y'know... in here. Taught me a lot. Not just the knowledge. Way he carried himself.

CON: *(To RAY.)* See? This is what I'm talking about.

RAY: *(To ANTHONY.)* My brother tell you to say all this, did he?

ANTHONY: No.

RAY: Cos it's all a little bit... scripted, know what I mean?

ANTHONY: I just come cos Hawkins said I could get something. From the room.

RAY: Yeah, you said.

ANTHONY: *(To CON.)* I think he... I think he knew. Like, he'd made his mind up. What he did. Knew that his time was... y'know? Limited.

CON: Did you... I mean, you couldn't have just done the knowledge for six hours a day. In here. That would be insane. Wouldn't it?

ANTHONY: Man had stamina.

CON: For eighteen months though?

ANTHONY: He was like a bull, you get me? He'd just keep going.

CON: I know it's what you *did* in here, I'm not saying that, but –

ANTHONY: There was no let up, you get me?

CON: But there must've been times... he musta talked about other... stuff. I mean, he must've mentioned, for example, he and I, that we... well, we fell out?

ANTHONY: No, not really.

CON: That we, y'know...

ANTHONY: What?

CON: Because I was meaning to come round. To his flat. Not here, I didn't know about this place, like I said on the phone I wasn't aware of... Cos you know, he could be a stubborn...

ANTHONY: He could, yeah.

CON: Couldn't he? I bet you found that in here. Bet he was a hard taskmaster, cracking the whip...

ANTHONY: Well, this is it.

CON: Did he... like, in passing, did he ever say what happened between us?

ANTHONY: Not really, no.

CON: Come on, Anthony, must've said something.

ANTHONY: He was a bit private like that.

CON: Kept himself to himself you mean?

ANTHONY: Something like that, yeah.

Beat. CON nods, to himself.

CON: But he must've said something, Anthony. *(Beat.)* In passing. In here. Yeah? Must've just –

ANTHONY: No. He never did. That's what I'm saying.

CON: But *you* knew about us, surely. About me and Ray. This is Ray, by the way.

RAY: Hello.

ANTHONY: Alright, Ray? You look smaller than you do on the telly.

CON: Well, he never really got on with Ray, you see, so he might not have mentioned –

ANTHONY: He said that he didn't have a family.

CON: Excuse me?

ANTHONY: That he didn't have a family.

CON: He said that?

ANTHONY: Yeah.

CON: To you.

ANTHONY: That's what he told me, yeah.

CON: What?

ANTHONY: Well, just that. So when you phoned...

CON: Whoa whoa whoa. But how did he... how did the subject... what did he say exactly? Like, think about this a sec, the exact words, how did he –

ANTHONY: He said that he was on his own.

CON: You mean he said that we fell out.

ANTHONY: No.

CON: That I hadn't been round to see him in –

ANTHONY: No, he never mentioned that. He just said that he didn't have any family. That he never had a family.

CON: He said that to you.

ANTHONY: Yeah.

CON: He confided that to you.

ANTHONY: Yeah.

CON: In here. To you.

ANTHONY: So it's a bit of a surprise, all this. To be honest. You lot.

PEGGY: I'll bet.

ANTHONY: Actually, tell a lie, that's not strictly true.

RAY: Oh, you missed a bit out did you?

ANTHONY: He told me he did have a family once.

RAY: Oh, did he?

ANTHONY: When he was in Boston.

CON: Boston. *(To PEGGY.)* Can you believe this?

ANTHONY: Yeah, back in the day. Like, fifty years ago or something.

CON: He was never in Boston, Anthony.

ANTHONY: Well, actually he was. I think.

PEGGY: According to who?

ANTHONY: According to him.

CON: He was never, ever, in his life, in –

ANTHONY: I'm only telling you what he told me, mate.

RAY: This is new information for you then, Con?

CON: Shut up, Ray. So what happened in Boston then?

ANTHONY: He was a good bloke.

CON: Yeah, you said that.

ANTHONY: What he taught me in here… He turned my life around. No one ever took the time to teach me –

CON: Yeah, we got all that, Anthony…

ANTHONY: Didn't want to get into this.

PEGGY: Into what?

ANTHONY: Look, he's obviously told me a few fibs and he's not given me the whole –

CON: What happened to this family in Boston?

ANTHONY: I only knew the geezer when I was in here learning the –

CON: What happened to the family in Boston?

ANTHONY: And I definitely didn't know about any of –

CON: What happened to this family in Boston then?

ANTHONY: They died.

CON: Died.

ANTHONY: That's what he said.

CON: Hear that, Ray? They died. This family in Boston.

ANTHONY: That's what he told me.

CON: When?

ANTHONY: *(To RAY.)* Look, thanks for helping out back there and that, but I didn't know about any –

CON: When?

ANTHONY: Years ago.

CON: Who? Who, Anthony?

ANTHONY: Boy and a girl. And his wife.

CON: How?

ANTHONY: Well, what he told me –

CON: How did they die?

ANTHONY: Fire.

CON: A house fire?

ANTHONY: Yeah. He said he went over... as a young man. Took the boat. Him and his wife. From Mullingar. To Dublin. Boat from there. Look, he's obviously told me a pack of –

CON: As what?

ANTHONY: I wasn't even listening to him properly half the time, mate, he was –

CON: As what?

ANTHONY: As a carpenter. Had his own company. Very successful, plenty of work, loads of men working for him. Said it was boom times back then, in Boston. Loved it there, he said. The air, kept going on about there being something in the air over there. The attitude of the people. The opportunities.

CON: And then there was this fire?

ANTHONY: That's what he said. Said they were all stuck in the house, on the second floor. He had a workshop in the basement, his offices. The door had jammed or something, they couldn't get the door... he lost everything. That's how he got that scar he said.

PEGGY: That scar on his –

ANTHONY: On his cheek. Caught it on a nail in the door. Trying to get them out.

RAY: That's how he got his scar, was it?

ANTHONY: That's what he told me, mate. That's when he came over here, after that.

CON: He told you he had no one over here?

ANTHONY: He said there'd been no one since the fire. Since Philomena.

CON: Who?

ANTHONY: His wife.

CON: Philomena. *(He looks at RAY.)* Don't laugh at me.

RAY: I wasn't.

CON: Don't you fucken laugh at me.

RAY: I wasn't laughing, Con.

CON: *(To ANTHONY, smiling.)* I can't make you out at all, Anthony.

ANTHONY: Hawkins just said I could –

CON: I invite you up here, to meet my brother, so you could tell him what you and my Dad did in here. Cos I thought that was a special thing. And I thought he should know about it.

ANTHONY: I didn't mean to upset you.

CON: Cos he didn't know that about Dad. What you did here. *We* didn't know it.

ANTHONY: Look, I just came for the –

CON: So why would you do that to me, Anthony?

ANTHONY: Do what?

CON: Why would you come here and tell me that, about my father, in front of my brother and my wife?

ANTHONY: Because that's what he said.

CON: Why would you lie like that?

RAY: He's not lying, Con.

CON: *(To RAY.)* Why would he come in here and mug us off with some swaggy story like that about the old man?

RAY: He's only repeating what the man said to him.

CON: I mean, what function does that serve?

RAY: He's not saying anything that –

CON: The man's *memory*?

RAY: Leave him be, Con…

CON: What the man *did* in here…?

PEGGY: Con, he didn't know…

CON: What the man *showed* him…?

PEGGY: He's only telling you what Mick –

CON: Taught him, nurtured him, cared for –

RAY: That's enough now, Con. Just –

CON: Fucken… fucken *loved* him?

RAY: It ain't his fault.

CON: Turns round… sticks a screwdriver in the man's heart, sticks a screwdriver in the man's memory? After everything he… after everything he…

He goes to ANTHONY.

Saw the mass card, didn't yer? Saw her name, saw that
woman's name, figured out the dates, figured out the…
didn't yer? Made up some… Philomena? My mum's
name… my mother's name was *Breda*. I don't know why
you did that, but that's… what you did, ent it? *(Beat.)* On
his cheek? On his fucken… ? Boston? He'd never even
been to Boston *Manor*. I mean, for Christ's sake, it's…

ANTHONY just stares at him.

*He turns slowly, and with deliberation, goes to the workbench on
the back wall. He retrieves a tatty red hardback notebook, which has
been concealed underneath it. With great care he wipes it, and tucks
it under his arm. He looks over to RAY.*

ANTHONY: Thanks for the milk and that.

*RAY nods. ANTHONY nods curtly at PEGGY and goes. The street
door slams, off.*

RAY: That's what you wanted to show me?

PEGGY: *(Softly.)* Don't, Ray.

RAY: No, I really thought I had the measure of the man.

PEGGY: Leave it.

RAY: He erased us! What a genius. I'd never have thought of
that.

PEGGY: Con, the state of mind he was in at the time…

RAY: Except *he* can't be erased, Con, can he?

PEGGY: Shut up, Ray.

RAY: Know how he got the scar, Peg? On his cheek. He did
catch it on a nail, actually. When he fell down the stairs. He
caught it on a nail that the, er… *calendar*

CON: *(Simultaneously with RAY, softly.)* … calendar…

RAY: was hanging by, on the back of the door to the living
room. He took a swing at me. Pissed. Lost his balance.

He can't be erased, Con, cos he's *indelible*.

CON: Yeah… and how you made it pay.

RAY: What're you talking about now?

CON: Your pain.

RAY: Did you hear what the kid just said? He would rather invent another family in another country than acknowledge us. That's the kind of man our father was. So you can tear down the shrine now, Con.

CON: Very lucrative, weren't it? Your one-man Greek tragedy.

RAY: I got out from under it, Con.

CON: Much better than trying to live through it, eh?

RAY: The man tried to destroy us.

CON: Who? Who did he –

RAY: We weren't ever part of that life he imagined for himself.

CON: But he was never that way with me, Ray. If he tried to destroy you why didn't he try to destroy –

RAY: Because you were his *accomplice.*

CON: Accomplice?

RAY: It happened because you let it, Con.

CON: Let what? What did I –

RAY: And I don't blame you, cos you couldn't know that you were doing that. But it happened cos of you.

CON: I was your kid brother. You left me there. How could I possibly –

RAY: Because you helped him build it. The myth. You were his audience. He was playing just for you. You did it together.

CON: What're you on about, Ray?

RAY: Mum was carrying me when they came over. I was the reason they left Ireland. That's why they married. That's how it was then.

CON: Bollocks.

RAY: No, Mum told me.

CON: When?

RAY: Years ago.

CON: Bollocks.

RAY: I shoulda told you, Con.

CON: Bollocks.

RAY: But I couldn't. I couldn't take away what he was from you. I didn't have the right to do that.

CON: He did something here.

RAY: He'd taken you to Millwall. A league game. It was pissing down. I was sat at the kitchen table. She'd just made me a cup of tea. She stood at the sink looking out the window. Her face like flayed meat, way the light caught it. Didn't look at me. Said it like she was reading out the football results. Cos it shouldn't have been her, she said. It was never meant to be her and it was never meant to be England. It was always supposed to be Philomena.

CON: But she died. *(To PEGGY.)* I remember now, what it was. The three of them. She died and –

RAY: No. She died after that, Con. After they came here. In that canal in Mullingar. Aged eighteen. They were all friends, Mum said. You're right about that.

CON: And they split up and –

RAY: No, they hadn't. They hadn't split. She was going over to America after her leaving cert, and he was going to join her. It was always supposed to be Boston. Mick and Philomena. It was always supposed to be her.

CON: Why would he... why wouldn't he just say? Nah. Throw his life away cos of a...?

RAY: You weren't part of any of that, Con. You weren't tainted with it. You were clean.

Beat.

CON: His face. When he looked up at me. Last time I… down at his old place, just off Walworth road, last time I saw him… He just wanted me to be with… I turned my back on him and –

PEGGY: Con…

CON: You didn't see what was in his eyes, Peggy. All red and blistered and… Doesn't make sense. Why would he –

PEGGY: I don't know, Con. I don't know.

CON is staring at her. Beat.

CON: Yeah. I went in the cab. Cos I was going on to do my shift straight after. Twelve, one o'clock. About then. Thought I'd get a cuppa tea, sandwich, before I… y'know. Brought him over some back copies of the Boxing News. He used to like the section on old timers. It's just hello and goodbye, Dad, just dropping these off, I'll call round after I knock off. Come in, he goes. Nah, I'll crack on, Dad. Want to get started. Come on, son, five minutes. No, don't want to get back too late, I promised the girls. Five minutes. I'd been starting later and later, cos I'd always end up sleeping off a, er… Five minutes, son. That's all he –

PEGGY: Just tell him.

CON: Didn't even fill the kettle, didn't even pretend to stick it on. Out comes the Powers. Two glasses. Can't do it, Dad. I can't be around it, you know that. Pours 'em out. Break the bread with me, Con. Look, Dad, I explained all this, you know that I can't be around that, you know that… Slides the glass over. And I'd been good. I'd started going to meetings regular, I'd… The toast is: To my two beautiful grand daughters. Dad, I'm driving. Got the cab parked outside, I'm working, I'm going out now on the… You refusing the toast, Con? The toast is… Dad, I'm just about to start my… You refusing to sup with me, now, Con? You not gonna toast my two lovely, beautiful grand daughters with me? Shoulda left the cab there…

PEGGY: He knew what he was doing, love.

CON: That was the thing, shoulda rang Dennis, for a lift back. Shoulda just slept it off…

RAY: He got what he wanted, Con.

CON: How is it what he wanted? How is sending me out on the road in that state what he wanted?

PEGGY: He did it deliberately, Con.

CON: Yeah, but I didn't have to take the drink, did I? Didn't pour it down my… It doesn't make any… Why would he… ? He wouldn't have done that to me, he was my best friend, he wouldn't have… he didn't make me actually drive the…

Silence. RAY goes to him and holds him tightly.

RAY: Let him go, mate. Let him go.

He holds him firmly for a while. Silence.

They disengage.

I should, er…

CON: *(Nodding.)* Straight up the Cut to Waterloo. Bakerloo to Paddington.

RAY: Right.

CON is staring at the floor. Beat.

RAY: I'm Sparticus.

CON: *(Dully, barely audible.)* No, I'm…

RAY: Oh yeah. Didn't recognise you in that light.

RAY extends the handle of his Samsonite suitcase. PEGGY embraces him.

PEGGY: Don't be a stranger, Ray.

RAY: Think about what I said, Peg.

PEGGY: Yeah.

He goes to the door, turns.

RAY: Fusion cuisine. I have seen the future.

He goes. The street door slams, off. Beat.

CON: What did that mean?

PEGGY: What?

CON: Think about what I said.

She stares at him a moment.

PEGGY: Nothing. I should pick the girls up from Mum's. She'll be going mental. I'll get the car. I'll pick the girls up and swing by on the way back.

CON: You sure?

PEGGY: Yeah. I've been thinking about the restaurant idea, the bistro.

CON: Oh yeah?

PEGGY: Maybe we should park it. For a bit.

CON: Oh, yeah, because I didn't actually get to ask Ray about the money, love. Didn't find the right moment to… It didn't seem…

PEGGY: I was going off the idea a bit anyway.

CON: Yeah, financially it's a bit…

PEGGY: *(She picks up her bag and starts to look through it.)* Yeah.

CON: Lose something?

PEGGY: *(Finds what she's looking for.)* No, got it. See you in a bit.

CON: He was here alone.

PEGGY: That's how he chose it, Con.

She goes. Beat. The street door slams.

CON is staring at the cab. He goes to it, runs his finger along the wheel arch. He crouches to pick up the box of memorabilia and starts to put the CDs and paraphernalia into it. As he does so, he selects a

CD and inserts it. He plays it. It plays The Fields Of Athenry, *by* The Dubliners.

He stands very still, listening down into himself a moment. He turns to continue collecting items on the table together and sees the bottle of Powers there. He goes out the back and returns a moment later with a glass. He picks up the bottle, unscrews it, pours a glass. He places the glass down, regarding it at length. He picks it up. He puts it down. Stares at it. He picks it up, toasts the jacket hanging on the nail, unscrews the bottle and pours the whiskey back in, wiping any spilt fluid on his trousers.

He snaps off the music, unplugs the stereo, and bundles it into the cardboard box. He continues to collect together the paraphernalia in the room.

The lights snap to black.

www.ingramcontent.com/pod-product-compliance
Ingram Content Group UK Ltd.
Pitfield, Milton Keynes, MK11 3LW, UK
UKHW020725280225
455688UK00012B/520